徐志摩

Xu Zhimo

Selected Poems

EDITED BY NICOLE CHIANG

OLEANDER PRESS

The Oleander Press
16 Orchard Street
Cambridge
CB1 1JT

www.oleanderpress.com

This Edition © The Oleander Press 2012.
English translations © The Oleander Press
Introduction © Lai-Sze Ng

A CIP catalogue record for the book is
available from the British Library.

ISBN: 9780900891694

Printed in England

TABLE OF CONTENTS

ENGLISH POEMS TRANSLATED BY XU ZHIMO

Matthew Arnold

Christina Rossetti

INTRODUCTION

More than a turning point in his life, Xu Zhimo's (1897–1931) Cambridge experience is pivotal in producing and shaping one of the most romantic writers in modern China. Xu created a literary Cambridge that, more than any other foreign places that were portrayed in modern Chinese literature, is Chinese readers' "dreamland" of the West. When the native Chinese Xu addressed Cambridge as "xiang" (native place), how should we see Xu's nostalgia for his second homeland? Through his Cambridge works, Xu created a perceived image of the place to his readers, and this image possessed an aura that stood the test of time and space, which we would term as "chronotopic aura".

If Shaoxing of China is identified with Lu Xun, West Hunan with Shen Congwen and Beijing with Lao She, then the mention of Xu Zhimo (1897–1931) will invoke the image of Cambridge among readers of modern Chinese literature. In fact, the most celebrated work of Xu is his poem entitled "Farewell again, Cambridge" (再别康桥), which has been included in Chinese literature textbooks around Asia, such as Singapore and Taiwan.

Unlike many of the May Fourth realist writers whose magnum opus are often set in their homeland in China, the romantic writer Xu composed many of his great works on foreign land, like "Scraps of Paris" (巴 黎的鳞爪). Xu's frequent overseas travel could be traced to his family's affluence. With the expectation that his son would continue the family banking business, Xu's father sent him overseas to study banking at Clark University in America in 1918. Later, Xu went on to Columbia University and the London School of Economics in 1919 and 1920, respectively. However, it was only during his short stint in Cambridge from 1921 to 1922 that Xu was inspired to seriously write modern poetry. The majority of Xu's Cambridge works were written after he returned to China, such as poems "Spring" (春, 1922), "Wild west Cambridge at dusk" (康桥西野暮色, 1922), "Farewell to Cambridge" (再会吧！康桥, 1922), "Farewell again, Cambridge" (1928), and a prose "The Cambridge I know" (我所知道的康桥,1926).

Xu once declared that Cambridge was his best overseas study experience and in his prose, "The Cambridge I know", even addressed Cambridge as "xiang" (native place). How should we see Xu's nostalgia for his second homeland? Was it really Cambridge he missed or was it the loss of a part of himself that had evoked this nostalgia? Furthermore, through his works on Cambridge, Xu created a perceived image of the place to his readers, and this image possessed an aura that stood the test of time and space, which I wish to term as "chronotopic aura." In this essay, I will attempt to analyse Xu Zhimo's Cambridge experience that evoked his nostalgia and also propose a new reading of Xu's works on Cambridge in terms of the chronotopic aura between literary Cambridge and its readers.

Prior to Cambridge, Xu had studied in Massachusetts, New York and London, majoring in history, French or Economics. Although Xu obtained first class honours at Clark University, there is no record reflecting his love for his studies then. In Unpublished Diaries of Xu Zhimo (徐志摩未刊日记), "Diary written in the States" (留美日记) records his response to events in China, particularly the May Fourth Movement. This diary, written in 1919, is heavy in its political slant, contrasting with "Diary written in Britain" (留英日记), a record of profound personal emotions.

Xu went to England in 1920 "to be a follower of Russell." However, his hopes were shattered as upon arrival, the philosopher Bertrand Russell (1872-1970) had just been ousted from Trinity College of Cambridge University. After studying half a year in the London School of Economics, Xu finally managed to enroll in Cambridge as a "special student" at King's College, through the arrangement of Cambridge historian Goldsworthy Dickinson (1862-1932).

Returning to China after a one-year stint in Cambridge, Xu published "The Cambridge I know" in Chenbao fukan (Supplement of Chenbao) in 1926, in which he notably employed the word "nostalgia" (思乡) when recollecting his Cambridge days. While "sixiang" means the sentimental recollection of one's native place, there are in fact two tiers of nostalgia Xu experienced – the Cambridge experience, and his "past self" in Cambridge.

Soon after Xu arrived in Spring 1921, his then-wife Zhang Youyi joined him in Sawston, a small town southwest of Cambridge. For the entire spring, he led a mundane life: "I was still a stranger in Cambridge, with no acquaintances –I have yet to taste the Cambridge life. All I knew was a library, some classrooms and eateries that sell cheap meals." It was only from that autumn after Zhang Youyi left did he have "the opportunity to live the real Cambridge life." One vital event took place alongside his discovery of

Cambridge – the discovery of himself and his literary identity. Leo Lee calls it a "spiritual rebirth" – a new sense of identity after a long period of "moratorium in China and the United States." Amidst setbacks in his love life (he divorced Zhang Youyi in March 1922 but received no affirmation from his lover, Lin Huiyin), Xu underwent a momentous transformation in his intellectual and literary pursuits, as he argues: "My eyes are opened by Cambridge. My desire for knowledge is stirred by Cambridge. My self-consciousness takes its embryonic form in Cambridge." In fact, the discovery of Cambridge is the discovery of the Self.

As a "special student" who could sit in for any subject, Xu attained his much cherished freedom: active intellectual engagement free of examinations. Consequently, he spent his time taking long strolls, smoking, discussing and drinking afternoon teas with English friends. To begin with, Cambridge is a unique town with an assembly of intellectuals. It was not his only overseas institution, yet Xu singled out Cambridge's greatest significance:

> I spent two years in America, and two years in England... If I was a pure dunce when I came to America, I remained unchanged when I left the Goddess of Liberty. But if I was unenlightened in America, my days at Cambridge at least made me realize that previously I was full of ignorance. This difference is by no means little.

Leo Lee argues that the "intrusion" of literati G.L. Dickinson, E.M. Forster and new-found love Lin Huiyin had gradually steered Xu's "path" to literature. Association with these "British gentlemen of repute" too played a significant role in guiding him to "self-discovery." Besides being a close acquaintance, Dickinson had a great impact on Xu's life. In his letter to artist-critic Roger Fry, Xu admits: "I have always thought it the greatest occasion in my life to meet Mr. Dickinson. It is due to him that I could have come to Cambridge and been [sic] enjoying all these happy days; that my interest in literature and arts began to shape and perpetuate itself."

Through Dickinson, Xu got to know Roger Fry and other English writers, Edward Carpenter, Katherine Mansfield and L.A. Richards. Although Xu's initial plan to "follow Russell" did not materialized, his admiration for Russell intensified after attending Russell's talks in the Cambridge Heretics' Club (a discussion group for philosophers). These acquaintances and activities during his Cambridge days highlighted his "pure belief". This "pure belief," according to Hu Shi, consists of "Love, Freedom and Beauty", and Xu's pursuit of these ultimate goals from his Cambridge days formed the basis not only of his literary self, but his true self – "xingling" (innate sensibility).

The concept of "xingling" is the most distinctive characteristics of the Gong'an school of poetry and has become the hallmark of its leader, Yuan Hongdao's (1568-1610) literary theory. Yuan maintains that one should "uniquely express [one's] personality and innate sensibility without being restrained by convention and form".

9

"Xingling" is specifically mentioned by Xu in "The Cambridge I know":

> ...listening to the sounds of water under starlight, listening to the sounds of night bells in nearby village, listening to the mooing of tired cows at the riverside, is one of the most magical experiences I have in Cambridge: the beauty of nature, serenity, harmonize in the privities of this starlight and light of the wave, by chance flood into your *innate sensibility*.

Xu's "xingling" can be seen as a convergence of the external Cambridge environment and his internal spiritual realm – which takes both the form of a temperament and an unconventional manner of expressing this temperament. Not only does the idyllic environ of Cambridge provoke a sublimation effect, it forcefully "floods" his consciousness and emotions, so much so that his inner sensibility harmonizes with the slow- paced, reclusive atmosphere of Cambridge. This innate sensibility is then translated into his works as they are "unconstrained by specific styles or conventions" technically. For instance, Xu's poetry did not adhere to specific poetics such as the standardised classical or the totally free-versed modern forms, but selectively inherited the emphases on rhythm and structure from classical poetry, techniques from Western poetics, and the vernacular language from modern Chinese literary movement. An example would be "Farewell again, Cambridge." Content-wise, he allows his Cambridge experience to be "flown from his thoughts and feelings," to capture his experience in the pursuit of love, freedom and beauty.

In his Cambridge works, Xu describes the beauty of River Cam and its surroundings, the famous "backs," the spring and the tranquility at dusk. However, his works such as "Tattling while living in the mountains of Firenze" (翡冷翠山居闲话), also focus on nature, which are not dissimilar from Cambridge. In fact, his Cambridge works sometimes pale in terms of foreign experiences and interpersonal encounters. But what stands out in his Cambridge works is the Self he portrays – a debonair and unrestrained poet who quietly takes his leave from Cambridge and "flicks his sleeves without bringing away a wisp of cloud", and a carefree youth who devotes himself to the beauty of nature. This state of life coincides with what Xu relishes – his pure belief; in particular, his freedom and carefree Self.

Xu repeatedly emphasizes the importance of solitude. In "The Cambridge I know", he writes:

> If you want to discover your true self, you have to give yourself an opportunity to be alone. If you want to discover a place (which may also be spiritual), you would also need to have a chance to play alone.

Notice that Xu's solitary self precedes his appreciation of a locality. Hence, the inner states of aloneness and selfhood at Cambridge are later dearly missed by him. In "Another self-dissection" (再自剖), Xu claims that to evade the state of depression, he has to attain "loneliness", which is precisely what Cambridge offers – absolute solitariness.

However, this state of solitude was burdened by realities after he returned to China in August 1922. His grandmother demise was followed by the death of close acquaintance Lin Changmin and his second son. His lover Lin Huiyin married Liang Sicheng, and his new love, Lu Xiaoman, was already married. Political upheavals in China also contradicted with his yearning for peace. Lastly, "Creation Society" and Lu Xun harshly criticised his editorial stance and poetics. Xu's essays, such as "Self-dissection" (自剖,1926), reflected such misery:

> Previously, when I see the golden waves glittering in the sunlight, it was as if seeing the immortal or the imperial palace – incredible and beautiful hallucination would sweep past my mind; but it is different now, sunlight is merely sunlight, flowing waves are merely flowing waves, no matter how splendid, it cannot affect my dull heart anymore.

Such writings contrast strikingly with his Cambridge writings, in which, for instance in "Wild west Cambridge at dusk", a star is like a light boat sailing through the clouds. Another essay, "Consulting a doctor" (求医), expresses his fear of being misunderstood and the desire to escape from the worldly miseries. It is significant that at the end of the essay, he quotes from Mansfield to echo his innermost feelings. It seems that when despondency dawn on him, Xu turns not to his immediate surroundings but to his Cambridge days, the intellectuals that had inspired him and to the state of the past self. Though I would not go as far as critic Zhao Xiaqiu who contends that upon return to China, Xu's "pure belief" gradually turns to doubt, I would argue that the tension caused by the disjuncture between his strongly held beliefs and the external situations accounts for his 'self-nostalgia' and longing for Cambridge days, when both the external environ and his inner self achieved a high degree of harmony.

The above argument thus sums up the complicated state of nostalgia Xu experienced when he mentioned the word "sixiang". His nostalgia for Cambridge comes in two tiers, firstly, the possibilities that Cambridge had given him, in particular, the discovery of his true self; secondly, he was also subconsciously missing his previous self in Cambridge.

Xu's works on Cambridge are permeated with highly intense emotions, filtering out any despondency – what remains is joy and hope. Consequently, the Cambridge he portrays evokes romantic and heavenly imagination. Significantly, Xu crafts a Cambridge that is literary, representational and atemporal, therefore thrusting into his readers a great sense of desire to, not only visit Cambridge, but to visit Xu's Cambridge. This creates a Cambridge that is imaginary or literary. This literary Cambridge does not come by easy as

Xu discloses in "The Cambridge I know":

> When someone has to write of his most beloved, be it someone or somewhere, it is the most difficult task. You are afraid of portraying a wrong picture, or to provoke it by overdoing it, you are afraid you will not do it justice by being reticent.

Xu is in fact worried about the loss of aura when reconstructing Cambridge–his literary Cambridge. Henceforth, to write the unwritable – his past impressions on Cambridge without losing aesthetic distance, Xu brilliantly creates what I would like to term as a chronotopic aura between the literary Cambridge and its readers.

A term coined by Mikhail Bakhtin, chronotope literally means "time-space". The concept is based on the idea that spatial and temporal dimensions are inseparable in works of literature. Next, aura is the term used by Walter Benjamin to describe the mystical sense that surrounds artistic or ritual objects – the "semblance of distance" which gives an object a human presence as though it would look back at its viewer. By saying that Xu has created a chronotopic aura between literary Cambridge and its readers, I mean that not only does he deliberately inject a 'aesthetic distance' by creating a mystical and artistic distance between the literary subject and its audience, he, intentionally or unintentionally, further compounds such 'distancing effects' by a protraction of the spatial and temporal gaps, both of which are inseparable, between his writings and his intended readers.

Firstly, the aesthetic distance is created by his dexterous use of imagery and rhetoric. In "Farewell Again, Cambridge": "The golden willows by the riverside/Are brides in the setting sun/.../The creek under the elm tree/Holds not water but the rainbow from the sky", metaphors used – brides and rainbow – are not only beautiful and romantic in nature, but also desirable yet unattainable, hence evoking imaginations in the readers' minds. Another poem "Wild West Cambridge at dusk" writes: "The sunglow is in the woods and fields/The sunglow is in the open country and deep in the brook/The sunglow is chasing in the front and back of the wind/The sunglow is between the eyebrows of the village girl/The sunglow is at the throat of the swallow and the back of the crow/The sunglow is hovering in the crowing of the cockerel and the barking of the dogs " The sun's glow is constantly spreading from the woods to the girl, and to farm animals. Readers are mesmerized by these descriptions which, more than performing the rhetorical function of depicting the picturesque sceneries, create sceneries more stunning than the reality. With such powerful rhetoric, a realm that resembles scholar-critic Wang Guowei's (1877-1927) concept of jingjie (realm – an idealistic world internally constructed by artist and portrayed by art after continuous aesthetic pursuits) is created.

Secondly, the aesthetic gap Xu creates in his works is amplified by the spatial distance between Britain and China. Cambridge is geographically far from Xu's intended Chinese readers in China [his works were submitted to *Shishi xinbao, Chenbao, Xiaoshuo yuebao*]. Thus when they were led by Xu's poetic portrayal to gaze at the distant Cambridge, they were likely to conjure up a utopian image. As these works were published during the May Fourth Period when intellectuals carried forth the task of social "enlightenment", any information on the West and overseas studies was highly valued. While another May Fourth writer Yu Dafu's fiction based in Japan created a bleak overseas study experience, Xu's academic and idyllic experience was not only rare; the utopian-like image of Cambridge glorified and romanticized his experience. When the portrayal of Cambridge corresponds to the ideal image of overseas studies and the reader's personal yearning, it is as if the reader's gaze is reciprocated by the "returning gaze" of the distant Cambridge, thus making it more meaningful. As such gazes and returning gazes are further augmented by the insurmountable physical distance apart, Xu's Cambridge becomes all the more desirable and romanticized.

Thirdly, we look at the temporal aspect of Xu's writings. His Cambridge works were written between 1922 and 1928. Since their publications, almost a century has passed. In reality, the temporal distance between the reading and the writing can only continue to increase with time. However, we need not quantify such temporal distance in terms of years as Xu has successfully crafted a literary Cambridge that is crystallized in words and is atemporal. Most apparently, there are no time-specific events and historical narratives in these works that would invalidate them over time. Furthermore, Xu's descriptions of Cambridge, such as the beauty of the backs, the willow, the seasons and the activities like punting and leisure strolling, as well as the colleges, are still highly definitive of Cambridge.

Despite the changes to the 'real' Cambridge – the new town planning, pollution of River Cam, commercialization of punting, reconstruction of bridges or even restoration of the King's Chapel – Chinese readers associate the 'real' Cambridge directly with the literary Cambridge depicted by Xu. The following observations was made in the Summer of 2005: Pointing to St John's College, a Chinese tour guide was overheard telling Chinese tourists that was Xu Zhimo's college (to some, it is probable that every college belongs to Xu). Another group of Chinese tourists in front of Trinity College were self-declaring to be "taking photograph with Xu Zhimo's Cambridge." If Xu's literary Cambridge is crystallized in words, it has been further crystallized in photographs. "Xu Zhimo's Cambridge" is then another name for the literary Cambridge which these tourists first set out to visit, and eventually convinced that they have visited the 'real' Cambridge. From the tourists' enthusiasm in works like "Farewell again, Cambridge", this literary Cambridge must have stood the test of time as it continuously renders itself meaningful to tourists and readers. In this sense, Xu's literary Cambridge can be seen to be constantly maintaining a dialogical relationship with, or reciprocating the gaze back at, the reader from the distant 1920s. In essence, temporal aura is eternalized.

While highlighting the space-time chronotopic aura created by Xu as an important factor in "eternalizing" his works, it should be pointed out that there are other indirect yet significant factors. I have mentioned Hu Shi's summation of Xu's "real temperament" (zhen xingqing) – the pursuit of love, beauty and freedom. Xu's temperament in its purest form is reflected in his writings, such as "degrading" himself to be a waterweed in "Farewell again, Cambridge". And in describing a sunset he witnessed in "The Cambridge I know", Xu was so touched that he even knelt down before the magnificence – such naiveté and genuine purity is unconventionally and uniquely appealing.

According to Xu's teacher, the reformist-scholar Liang Qichao (1873-1929), Xu is "too frivolous". It could be due to this spirited, self-willed personality that Xu leads a legendary life with several romances under his name – some widely perceived as scandalous, such as his divorce with his first wife and the marriage with Lu Xiaoman (whose own divorce was the result of their affair). However, this romantic image not only superimposes on to the romantic Cambridge he portrays, his love life has been used, or even exploited, by the media. In 2000, a highly popular China-Taiwan TV drama serial based on Xu's life story, "April Rhapsody", was released. In a way, the serial revitalized the glamour of Xu and Cambridge. Additionally, the pathos which the TV serial adds to Xu's image, especially after his unexpected tragic death in the 1931 plane crash, contributes to the continuous attraction of Xu's Cambridge writings.

"Before the age of 24, my interest in poetry fell far below that of my interest on the theory of relativity or "The Social Contract"...my highest ambition was to become China's Hamilton! Before the age of 24, poetry, be it new or old, was totally irrelevant to me. If a person like me would really become a poet – what else is there to say?" This famous statement written by Xu in the Preface of his poetry collection Menghu Ji, gives us an important insight of the beginning of Xu's poetic career. Xu was 24 in 1920, the year when he went to England. More than a turning point in Xu's life, Cambridge is pivotal in shaping one of the most romantic writers in modern China. In turn, Xu returns the favour by creating a literary Cambridge that, more than any foreign place, is Chinese readers' "dreamland".

Lai-Sze Ng
Jurong Junior College, Singapore
May 2012

ORIGINAL
POEMS

By Chance

I am a cloud in the sky,
By chance projecting a shadow on the wave of your heart
Don't be surprised,
No need to be elated;
In an instant I shall vanish without trace.

We come across each other in a dark night on the sea,
You on your way, I on mine.
Remember if you will,
Or, better still, forget
The light exchanged in this encounter.

偶然

我是天空里的一片云
偶尔投影在你的波心
　　你不必讶异
　　更无须欢喜
在转瞬间消灭了踪影

你我相逢在黑夜的海上
你有你的　我有我的　方向
　　你记得也好
　　最好你忘掉
在这交会时互放的光亮

Go!

Go, living world, go!
I stand alone on the mountain summit;
Go, living world, go!
I face the boundless skies.

Go, youth, go!
Bury yourself with the fragrant herbs of the valleys;
Go, youth, go!
Turning over sorrow to the sunset's crows

Go, dream haven, go!
I shatter the jade cup of beautiful illusions;
Go, dream haven, go!
I smile and accept the felicitations of the mountain winds
        and the roaring seas.

Go, this and that, go!
Right in front of you is a mountain piercing the sky!
Go, everything, go!
Right in front of you is never-ending eternity!

去吧

去吧，人间，去吧！
我独立在高山的峰上；
去吧，人间，去吧！
我面对着无极的穹苍。

去吧，青年，去吧！
与幽谷的香草同埋；
去吧，青年，去吧！
悲哀付与暮天的群鸦。

去吧，梦乡，去吧！
我把幻景的玉杯摔破；
去吧，梦乡，去吧！
我笑受山风与海涛之贺。

去吧，种种，去吧！
当前有插天的高峰；
去吧，一切，去吧！
当前有无穷的无穷！

It is Not Easy to Survive Nowadays

Yesterday I went to the Yanxia Mountains, visiting osmanthus
     flowers in a downpour;
The Southern Peaks were invisible in the mist.
In front of a thatched cottage,
I stopped to ask a country girl
Whether this year's osmanthus flowers at Wongjiashan were
     as fragrant as last year's.

The country girl looked me up and down.
as if looking at a soaked bird,
I supposed she must be feeling queer –
Walking along in torrential rain
For no reason, asking whether this year's osmanthus is
     aromatic or not.

"My guest, you are unlucky. You have come too late and
     too early.
This is the famous Manjianong Village,
Normally the aroma would be everywhere by now.
In the past few days, frequent rain and wind have made a mess,
Nearly all the early osmanthus flowers have wilted."

As expected, even a forest of osmanthus could not bring
     me cheer;
Only withered flower buds remained.
Dreary to look at. Alas, unexpected calamity.
Why is there languishment everywhere?
It is not easy to survive nowadays. It is not easy to
     survive nowadays!

这年头活着不易

昨天我冒着大雨到烟霞岭下访桂；
　　　南高峰在烟霞中不见，
　　　在一家松茅铺的屋檐前
　　　我停步，问一个村姑今年
翁家山的桂花有没有去年开的媚，

那村姑先对着我身上细细的端详；
　　　活象只羽毛浸瘪了的鸟，
　　　我心想，她定觉得蹊跷，
　　　在这大雨天单身走远道，
倒来没来头的问桂花今年香不香。

"客人，你运气不好，来得太迟又太早；
　　　这里就是有名的满家弄，
　　　往年这时候到处香得凶，
　　　这几天连绵的雨，外加风，
弄得这稀糟，今年的早桂就算完了。"

果然这桂子林也不能给我点子欢喜；
　　　枝上只见焦萎的细蕊，
　　　看着凄凄，唉，无妄的灾！
　　　为什么这到处是憔悴？
这年头活着不易！这年头活着不易！

Spring

The river is flowing slowly at sunset;
Evening clouds cling to tree crown and tree trunk.
Grasshoppers fly, grasshoppers playfully kiss the shining grass,
I'm looking while walking in the spring meadow.

Grasshoppers crouching on the chest of a flower;
The flower is so timid that it cannot stop shaking its head.
A soft pink hand stretches out from the grass,
Hugging the impetuous grasshoppers tight.

Golden plants, silver plants, scattering like stars
Embellish the welcoming grass.
The young couples on the green carpet
Murmuring lovers' prattle, lingering sentiments.

I nod and smile, walking towards the south,
Appreciating this green spring garden;
Trees chatting, grass communicating,
There is love and passion everywhere.

Sparrows joke frivolously in front of us,
People blush with love in the grassland.
I envy the couples,
But who envies my lonely lingering?

Lonely lingering,
Not that my heart is not excited and quivering;
Answering the call of youth,
Lighting up the splendid hope,
Oh, Spring! You are in my embrace.

春

河水在夕阳里缓流，
暮霞胶抹树干树头；
蚱蜢飞，蚱蜢戏吻草光光，
我在春草里看看走走。

蚱蜢匍伏在铁花胸前，
铁花羞得不住的摇头，
草里忽伸出之藕嫩的手，
将孟浪的跳虫拦腰紧拶。

金花菜，银花菜，星星澜澜，
点缀着天然温暖的青毡，
青毡上青年的情耦，
情意胶胶，情话啾啾。

我点头微笑，南向前走，
观赏这青透春透的园囿，
树尽交柯，草也骈偶，
到处是缱绻，是绸缪。

雀儿在人前猥盼亵语，
人在草处心欢面赧，
我羡他们的双双对对，
有谁羡我孤独的徘徊？

孤独的徘徊！
我心须何尝不热奋震颤，
答应这青春的呼唤，
燃点着希望灿灿，
春呀！你在我怀抱中也！

Saying Goodbye to Cambridge Again

Very quietly I take my leave
As quietly as I came here;
Quietly I wave goodbye
To the rosy clouds in the western sky.

The golden willows by the riverside
Are young brides in the setting sun;
Their reflections on the shimmering waves
Always linger in the depth of my heart.

The floating heart growing in the sludge
Sways leisurely under the water;
In the gentle waves of Cambridge
I would be a water plant!

That pool under the shade of elm trees,
Holds not water but the rainbow from the sky;
Shattered to pieces among the duckweeds,
Is the sediment of a rainbow-like dream.

To seek a dream? Just to punt a boat upstream
To where the green grass is more verdant;
Or to have the boat fully loaded with starlight,
To sing aloud in the splendour of starlight.

But I cannot sing aloud,
Quietness is my farewell music;
Even summer insects keep silence for me;
Cambridge is soundless tonight!

Very quietly I take my leave
As quietly as I came here;
Gently I flick my sleeves.
Not even a wisp of cloud will I bring away.

再别康桥

轻轻的我走了，
正如我轻轻的来；
我轻轻的招手，
作别西天的云彩。

那河畔的金柳，
是夕阳中的新娘；
波光里的艳影，
在我的心头荡漾。

软泥上的青荇，
油油的在水底招摇；
在康河的柔波里，
我甘心做一条水草！

那榆荫下的一潭，
不是清泉，是天上虹；
揉碎在浮藻间，
沉淀着彩虹似的梦。

寻梦？撑一支长篙，
向青草更青处漫溯；
满载一船星辉，
在星辉斑斓里放歌。

但我不能放歌，
悄悄是别离的笙箫；
夏虫也为我沉默，
沉默是今晚的康桥！

悄悄的我走了，
正如我悄悄的来；
我挥一挥衣袖，
不带走一片云彩。

Cricket

Cricket, why do you come here? The world
has long ceased to be its leisurely old self.
Green grass, white dew, are foolish too,
Useless stuff for verse!
Gold has taken pride of place,
It occupies the day, it rules dreams!
Love, like stars in the morning sky,
has long since withdrawn, vanished,
Even after nightfall they will not return:
Black cloud seals the heaven for ever.
Shame has taken long leave,
Found refuge in the desert.
Flowers bloom, but bear no fruit.
Thought is ravaged by creeds.
Don't say the days are filled with gloom –
There are darker still to come.
It is in part a indolence of soul,
Hiding in the garden, growing vegetables:
"I don't care," it says, " let things grow uglier still –
Turning into pigs, maggots, toads, dogs...
When the sun is too ashamed to shine,
The waning moon to wax,
When humanity is dead,
Then I will ring –
The bell of revolution!"

秋虫

秋虫，你为什么来？人间
早不是旧时候的清闲；
这青草，这白露，也是呆，
再也没有用，这些诗材！
黄金才是人们的新宠，
她占了白天，又霸住梦！
爱情：像白天里的星星，
她早就回避，早没了影。
天黑它们也不得回来，
半空里永远有乌云盖。
还有廉耻也告了长假，
他躲在沙漠地里住家；
花仅着开可结不成果，
思想被主义奸汙得苦！
你别说这日子过得闷，
晦气脸的还在后面跟！
这一半也是灵魂的懒，
他爱躲在园子里种菜
"不管，」他说:「听他往下丑——
变猪，变蛆，变蛤蟆，变狗……
过天太阳羞得遮了脸，
月亮残阙了再不肯圆，
到那天人道真灭了种，
我再来打——打革命的钟！"

I Don't Know Which Direction the Wind is Blowing

I don't know
Which direction the wind is blowing—
I am in a dream,
In the dream's gentle wave lingering.

I don't know
Which direction the wind is blowing —
I am in a dream,
Her tenderness, my fascination.

I don't know
Which direction the wind is blowing —
I am in a dream,
Sweetness is the glory of the dream.

I don't know
Which direction the wind is blowing —
I am in a dream,
Her betrayal, my depression.

I don't know
Which direction the wind is blowing —
I am in a dream,
heartbroken in the gloom of the dream.

I don't know
Which direction the wind is blowing —
I am in a dream,
Dimness is the glory of the dream.

我不知道风是在哪一个方向吹

我不知道风
是在哪一个方向吹 ——
我是在梦中,
在梦的轻波里依洄。

我不知道风
是在哪一个方向吹 ——
我是在梦中,
她的温存, 我的迷醉。

我不知道风
是在哪一个方向吹 ——
我是在梦中,
甜美是梦里的光辉。

我不知道风
是在哪一个方向吹 ——
我是在梦中,
她的负心, 我的伤悲。

我不知道风
是在哪一个方向吹 ——
我是在梦中,
在梦的悲哀里心碎。

我不知道风
是在哪一个方向吹 ——
我是在梦中,
黯淡是梦里的光辉。

Insignificance

I look up to the aged mountains,
They utter not a word.
The sunshine sketches out my insignificant being,
Grass shoots under my feet.

I stop on the verge of a path alone,
Listening to the soughing pines in the valley;
White clouds occupy the blue skies
And vanish in a blinking of an eye.

渺小

我仰望群山的苍老，
他们不说一句话。
阳光描出我的渺小，
小草在我的脚下。

我一人停步在路隅，
倾听空谷的松籁，
青天里有白云盘踞 --
转眼间忽又不在。

You Are in His Eyes

I climb the highest mountain,
My clothes are torn by thistles and thorns;
I stare at the misty sky –
Lord, I can't see you!

I dig into the hard crust,
Destroy the nest of the snakes and dragons;
I yell in the bottomless abyss –
Lord, I can't hear you!

I see a child by the side of the road,
A lively, pretty child with ragged clothes:
Calling his mum, his eyes shine with love –
Lord, you are in his eyes!

他眼里有你

我攀登了万仞的高冈，
荆棘扎烂了我的衣裳，
我向飘渺的云天外望——
上帝，我望不见你！

我向坚厚的地壳里掏，
捣毁了蛇龙们的老巢，
在无底的深潭里我叫——
上帝，我听不到你！

我在道旁见一个小孩，
活泼，秀丽，褴褛的衣衫；
他叫声妈，眼里亮着爱——
上帝，他眼里有你！

Wind in the Pines at Midnight

This is a hill in a winter's night,
An unfrequented temple at the foot of the hill,
A lonely soul inside the temple,
praying in repentance, sinking into despair.

Why this roaring, this howling,
Drum, gong, tiger and leopard?
Why this secret whisper, this personal admiration,
The tragedy of passion and the frustrations of life –
Once more like the tide, submerge
This hesitant soul and unfrequented temple?

夜半松风

这是冬夜的山坡,
坡下一座冷落的僧庐,
庐内一个孤独的梦魂:
在忏悔中祈祷,　在绝望中沉沦;---

为什么这怒叫,这狂啸,
鼍鼓与金钲与虎与豹?
为什么这幽诉,这私慕?
烈情的惨剧与人生的坎坷 ---
又一度潮水似的淹没了
这彷徨的梦魂与冷落的僧庐?

The Wide Sea

The wide sea or the empty sky I do not need.
I also do not want to make a big paper crane
Soaring above the sky teasing winds from all directions.
I only want one minute,
I only want a little light,
I only want a crack,
Crawling like a little child
In front of a window of a dark house,
Staring at the western sky for a
Crack, a little
Light, one
Minute.

阔的海

阔的海空的天我不需要，
我也不想放一只巨大的纸鹞
上天去捉弄四面八方的风；
我只要一分钟
我只要一点光
我只要一条缝，——
象一个小孩子爬伏在一间暗屋的窗前
望着西天边不死的一条
缝，一点
光，一分
钟。

A P'i-pa Tune in an Alley at Midnight

Again waking me up from a dream, a tune of p'i-pa in the
    still of the night!
Whose sorrowful thought,
Whose fingers,
Like a gust of chilly wind, a spell of depressing rain, and
    a shower of falling petals,
So late at night.
So drowsy the moment
The strumming of taut chords send forth disturbing notes
Blending into the night, the deserted street,
A waning moon hangs on top of the willow tree
Ah, the half-broken moon, like him whose hope has shattered. He
Wears a tattered cap,
And an iron chain,
Laughing and dancing on the path of time like mad
This is the end, he says, blow out your lamp,
She is waiting beyond her grave,
Waiting for you to kiss her,   Waiting for you to kiss her,   Waiting
    for you to kiss her

半夜深巷琵琶

又被它从睡梦中惊醒，深夜里的琵琶！
　　　是谁的悲思，
　　　是谁的手指，
像一阵凄风，像一阵惨雨，像一阵落花，
　　　在这夜深深时，
　　　在这睡昏昏时，
挑动着紧促的弦索，乱弹着宫商角徵，
　　　和着这深夜，荒街，
　　　柳梢头有残月挂，
啊，半轮的残月，像是破碎的希望他，他
　　　头戴一顶开花帽，
　　　身上带着铁链条，
在光阴的道上疯了似的跳，疯了似的笑，
　　　完了，他说，吹糊你的灯，
　　　她在坟墓的那一边等，
等你去亲吻，等你去亲吻，等你去亲吻。

English Poems Translated
by Xu Zhimo

The Tyger
by William Blake

Tyger, tyger, burning bright
In the forests of the night,
What immortal hand or eye
Could frame thy fearful symmetry?

In what distant deeps or skies
Burnt the fire of thine eyes?
On what wings dare he aspire?
What the hand dare seize the fire?

And what shoulder and what art
Could twist the sinews of thy heart?
And when thy heart began to beat,
What dread hand and what dread feet?

What the hammer? what the chain?
In what furnace was thy brain?
What the anvil? What dread grasp
Dare its deadly terrors clasp?

When the stars threw down their spears,
And water'd heaven with their tears,
Did He smile His work to see?
Did He who made the lamb make thee?

Tyger, tyger, burning bright
In the forests of the night,
What immortal hand or eye
Dare frame thy fearful symmetry?

猛虎

布雷克 著；徐志摩 译

猛虎，猛虎，火焰似的烧红
在深夜曲莽丛，
何等神明的巨眼或是手
能擘画你的骇人的雄厚？

在何等遥远的海底还是天顶
烧着你眼火的纯晶？
跨什么翅膀他胆敢飞腾？
凭什么手敢擒住那威棱？

是何等肩腕，是何等神通，
能摩楼你的藏府的系境？
等到你的心开始了活跳，
何等震惊的手，何等震惊的脚？

椎的是什么锤？使的是什么练？
在什么洪炉里熬炼你的脑液？
什么砧座？什么骇异的拿把
胆敢它的凶恶的惊怕擒抓？

当群星放射它们的金芒，
满天上氾滥着它们的泪光，
见到他的工程，他露不露笑容？
造你的不就是那造小羊的神工？

猛虎，猛虎，火焰似的烧红
在深夜的莽丛，
何等神明的巨眼或是手
胆敢擘画你的惊人的雄厚？

A Week
by Thomas Hardy

On Monday night I closed my door,
And thought you were not as heretofore,
And little cared if we met no more.

I seemed on Tuesday night to trace
Something beyond mere commonplace
In your ideas, and heart, and face.

On Wednesday I did not opine
Your life would ever be one with mine,
Though if it were we should well combine.

On Thursday noon I liked you well,
And fondly felt that we must dwell
Not far apart, whatever befell.

On Friday it was with a thrill
In gazing towards your distant vill
I owned you were my dear one still.

I saw you wholly to my mind
On Saturday — even one who shrined
All that was best of womankind.

As wing-clipt seagull for the sea
On Sunday night I longed for thee,
Without whom life were waste to me!

一个星期

哈代 著；徐志摩 译

星期一那天晚上我关上了我的门，
心想你满不是我心里的人，
此后见不见面都不关要紧。

到了星期二那晚上我又想到
你的思想，你的心肠，你的容貌，
到底不比得平常，有点儿妙。

星期三那晚上我又想起了你，
想你我要合成一体总是不易，
就说机会又叫你我凑在一起。

星期四中上我思想又换了样，
我还是喜欢你，我俩正不妨
亲近的住着，管它是短是长。

星期五那天我感到一阵心震 ，
当我望着你住的那个乡村，
说来你还是我亲爱的，我自认。

到了星期六你充满了我的思想，
整个的你在我心里发亮，
女性的美哪样不在你的身上？

像是只顺风的海鸥向着海飞，
到了星期天晚上我简直的发了迷，
还做什么人这辈子要没有你！

The Wound
by Thomas Hardy

I climbed to the crest,
And, fog-festooned,
The sun lay west
Like a crimson wound:

Like that wound of mine
Of which none knew,
For I'd given no sign
That it pierced me through.

伤痕

哈代 著；徐志摩 译

我爬上了山顶，
回望西天的光景，
太阳在云彩里
宛似一个血殷的伤痕；

宛似我自身的伤痕，
知道的没有一个人，
因为我不曾袒露隐秘，
谁知这伤痕透过我的心！

The Division
by Thomas Hardy

Rain on the windows, creaking doors,
With blasts that besom the green,
And I am here, and you are there,
And a hundred miles between!

O were it but the weather, Dear,
O were it but the miles
That summed up all our severance,
There might be room for smiles.

But that thwart thing betwixt us twain,
Which nothing cleaves or clears,
Is more than distance, Dear, or rain,
And longer than the years!

分离

哈代 著; 徐志摩 译

急风打着窗，震响的门枢，
　　大风呼呼的，狂扫过青草地，
在这里的我，在那里的你，
　　中间隔离着途程百里！

假如我们的离异，我爱，
　　只是这深夜的风与雨
只是这间隔着的百余里，
　　我心中许还有微笑的生机。

但在你我间的那个离异，我爱，
　　不比那可以短缩的距离，
不比那可以消歇的风雨，
　　更比那不尽的光阴，窈远无期！

Her Initials
by Thomas Hardy

Upon a poet's page I wrote
Of old two letters of her name;
Part seemed she of the effulgent thought
Whence that high singer's rapture came.
—When now I turn the leaf the same
Immortal light illumes the lay
But from the letters of her name
The radiance has died away.

她的名字

哈代 著; 徐志摩 译

在一本诗人的书页上
我画着她芳名的字形;
她像是光艳的思想的部分,
曾经灵感那歌吟者的欢欣。
如今我又翻着那张书页,
诗歌里依旧闪耀着光彩,
但她的名字的鲜艳,
却已随着过去的时光消淡。

To the Moon
by Thomas Hardy

"What have you looked at, Moon,
In your time,
Now long past your prime?"
"O, I have looked at, often looked at
Sweet, sublime,
Sore things, shudderful, night and noon
In my time."

"What have you mused on, Moon,
In your day,
So aloof, so far away?"
"O, I have mused on, often mused on
Growth, decay,
Nations alive, dead, mad, aswoon,
In my day!"

"Have you much wondered, Moon,
On your rounds,
Self-wrapt, beyond Earth's bounds?"
"Yea, I have wondered, often wondered
At the sounds
Reaching me of the human tune
On my rounds."

"What do you think of it, Moon,
As you go?
Is Life much, or no?"
"O, I think of it, often think of it
As a show
God ought surely to shut up soon,
As I go."

对月

哈代 著；徐志摩 译

"现在你是倦了老了的，不错，月，
　　　　　但在你年青的时候，
　　　你倒是看着了些个什么花头?"
"啊！我的眼福真不小，有的事儿甜，
　　　　　有的庄严，也有叫人悲愁，
　　黑夜，白天，看不完那些寒心事件，
　　　　在我年青青的时候。"

"你是那么孤高那么远，真是的，月，
　　　　　但在你年少的时光，
　　你倒是转着些个怎么样的感想?"
"啊我的感想，哪样不叫我低着头
　　　　　想，新鲜的变旧，少壮的亡，
民族的兴衰，人类的疯癫与昏谬，
　　　　　哪样不动我的感想?"

"你是远离着我们这个世界，月，
　　　　　但你在天空里转动，
有什么事儿打岔你自在的心胸?"
"啊，怎么没有，打岔的事儿当然有，
　　　　　地面上异样的徵角商宫，
说是人道的音乐，在半空里飘浮，
　　　　　打岔我自在的转动。"

"你倒是干脆发表一句总话，月，
　　　　　你已然看透了这回事，
人生究竟是有还是没有意思?"
"啊，一句总话，把它比作一台戏，
　　　　　尽做怎不叫人烦死，
上帝祂早该喝一声'幕闭'，
　　　　　我早就看腻了这回事。

I Look into My Glass
by Thomas Hardy

I look into my glass,
And view my wasting skin,
And say, "Would God it came to pass
My heart had shrunk as thin!"

For then, I, undistrest
By hearts grown cold to me,
Could lonely wait my endless rest
With equanimity.

But Time, to make me grieve,
Part steals, lets part abide;
And shakes this fragile frame at eve
With throbbings of noontide.

窥镜

哈代 著；徐志摩 译

我向着镜里端详，思忖，
镜里反映出我消瘦的身影。
我说："但愿仰上帝的慈恩，
使了我的心，变成一般的瘦损！"

因为枯萎了的心，不再感受
人们渐次疏淡我的寒冰，
我自此可以化石似的镇定，
孤独地，静待最后的安宁。

但不仁善的，磨难我的光阴，
消耗了我的身，却留着我的心；
鼓动着午潮般的脉搏与血运，
在昏夜里狂撼我消瘦了的身影。

The Meeting
by Katherine Mansfield

We started speaking,
Looked at each other, then turned away.
The tears kept rising to my eyes.
But I could not weep.
I wanted to take your hand
But my hand trembled.
You kept counting the days
Before we should meet again.
But both of us felt in our hearts
That we parted for ever and ever.
The ticking of the little clock filled the quiet room.
"Listen," I said. "It is so loud,
Like a horse galloping on a lonely road,
As loud as a horse galloping past in the night."
You shut me up in your arms.
But the sound of the clock stifled our hearts' beating.
You said, "I cannot go: all that is living of me
Is here for ever and ever."
Then you went.
The world changed. The sound of the clock grew fainter,
Dwindled away, became a minute thing.
I whispered in the darkness. "If it stops, I shall die."

会面

曼殊斐儿 著；徐志摩 译

你我说话了，
彼此望了望，又背转了身去。
眼泪不住的在我眼里升起
但我哭不出声，
我要把住你的手
但我的手在发着抖，
你尽算着日子
算过多少日子我们再能得见。
但你我在心里都觉得
我们这回分别了再也不得会面。
那只小钟的摆声充满了这静默的屋子。
"听呀，"我说。这声音响极了，
就像是一匹马在冷静的道上奔
有那样的闹——一匹马在夜里奔着过去。
你把我圈在你的臂围中。
但那钟的声音压住了我们心的跳动。
你说："我不能走，只要我是活着的，
永远永远和你一起在着。"
后来你去了。
世界变了相。钟的声音也是
越来越见软弱，衰萎了下去，
成了一件极不相干的事。
我在黑暗里低声说，
如果它停了，我就死。

The Gulf
by Katherine Mansfield

A Gulf of silence separates us from each other.
I stand at one side of the gulf, you at the other.
I cannot see you or hear you, yet know that you are there.
Often I call you by your childish name
And pretend that the echo to my crying is your voice.
How can we bridge the gulf?
Never by speech or touch.
Once I thought we might fill it quite up with tears.
Now I want to shatter it with our laughter.

深渊
曼殊斐儿 著；徐志摩 译

隔离着你我的是一个沉默的深渊。
我站在渊的这一边，你在那一边。
我见不到也听不到你，可知道你是在那里。
我再三提着你的小名儿呼唤你，
还把我也自己叫的回声当作你的答应。
我们如何填起这个深渊？
再不能用口，也不能用手。
我先前曾想我们许可以把眼泪
来填得它满满的。
现在我要用我们的笑声来
销毁了它。

Sleeping Together
by Katherine Mansfield

Sleeping together... how tired you were...
How warm our room... how the firelight spread
On walls and ceiling and great white bed!
We spoke in whispers as children do,
And now it was I – and then it was you
Slept a moment, to wake – "My dear,
I'm not at all sleepy," one of us said...

Was it a thousand years ago?
I woke in your arms – you were sound asleep –
And heard the pattering sound of sheep.
Softly I slipped to the floor and crept
To the curtained window, then, while you slept,
I watched the sheep pass by in the snow.

O flock of thoughts with their shepherd Fear
Shivering, desolate, out in the cold,
That entered into my heart to fold!

A thousand years... was it yesterday
When we two children of far away,
Clinging close in the darkness, lay
Sleeping together?... How tired you were....

在一起睡

曼殊斐儿 著；徐志摩 译

在一起睡；你倦得成个什么样子！
我们的屋子多么暖和；看这灯光
散落在板壁上，顶板上和大白床上！
我们像孩子似的低着声音说话，
一会儿是你，又一会儿是我，
睡了一晌又醒过来说——
亲爱的，我一点也不觉困，
不是你就是我说。
有一千年了吧？
我在你的怀抱中醒来——你睡得着着的——
我听得绵羊在走路的蹄声，
轻轻的我溜下了地，爬着走到
挂着帘子的窗口，
你还睡你的觉，
我望着一群羊在雪地里过去。
一群的思想，跟着他们的牧人"恐惧"。
颤抖着，在寒夜里凄凉的走着道，
它们走进了我的心窝如同羊进了圈！
一千年还不是昨天吗
我们俩，远远的两个孩子，
在黑暗中贴得紧紧的，
躺着在一起睡？
你倦得成个什么样子！

Tenebris Interlucentem V. II
by James Elroy Flecker

A linnet who had lost her way
Sang on a blackened bough in Hell,
Till all the ghosts remembered well
The trees, the wind, the golden day.
At last they knew that they had died
When they heard music in that land,
And some one there stole forth a hand
To draw a brother to his side.

有那一天

弗莱克 著; 徐志摩 译

她误入了地狱，一只梅花小雀，
歇在一株漆黑的树上，她唱，
她唱，唱醒了群鬼的怅惘，
怅惘清风，白日，青林的快乐。
唤醒了群鬼，这小鸟的声调，
这才明白他们已经来到地狱，
这时候有一只鬼手在摸索，
拉一个生前骨肉，紧紧地搂抱。

Requiescat
by Matthew Arnold

Trew on her roses, roses,
And never a spray of yew.
In quiet she reposes:
Ah! would that I did too.

Her mirth the world required:
She bathed it in smiles of glee.
But her heart was tired, tired,
And now they let her be.

Her life was turning, turning,
In mazes of heat and sound.
But for peace her soul was yearning,
And now peace laps her round.

Her cabin'd, ample Spirit,
It flutter'd and fail'd for breath.
To-night it doth inherit
The vasty hall of Death.

诔词

安诺德 著；徐志摩 译

散上玫瑰花，散上玫瑰花，
休搀杂一小枝的水松!
在寂静中她寂静的解化；
啊!但愿我亦永终。

她是个稀有的欢欣，人间
曾经她喜笑的洗净，
但倦了是她的心，倦了，可怜
这回她安眠了，不再苏醒。

在火热与扰攘的迷阵中
旋转，旋转着她的一生；
但和平是她灵魂的想望，　---
和平是她的了，如今。

局促在人间，她博大的神魂
何曾享受呼吸的自由；
今夜，在这静夜，她独自的攀登
那死的插天的高楼。

Song
by Christina Rossetti

When I am dead, my dearest,
Sing no sad songs for me;
Plant thou no roses at my head,
Nor shady cypress tree:
Be the green grass above me
With showers and dewdrops wet;
And if thou wilt, remember,
And if thou wilt, forget.

I shall not see the shadows,
I shall not feel the rain;
I shall not hear the nightingale
Sing on, as if in pain;
And dreaming through the twilight
That doth not rise nor set,
Haply I may remember,
And haply may forget.

歌

罗赛蒂 著; 徐志摩 译

当我死了的时候，亲爱的，
别为我唱悲伤的歌；
我坟上不必安插蔷薇
也无需浓荫的柏树；
让盖着我的轻轻的草
淋着雨，也沾着露珠；
假如你愿意，请记着我，
要是你甘心，忘了我。

我再不见地面的青荫，
觉不到雨露的甜蜜；
再听不到夜莺的歌喉，
在黑夜里倾吐悲啼；
在悠久的昏暮中迷惘，
阳光不升起也不消翳；
我也许，也许我记得你，
我也许，我也许忘记。

The Hour and the Ghost
by Christina Rossetti

BRIDE
O love, love, hold me fast,
He draws me away from thee;
I cannot stem the blast,
Nor the cold strong sea:
Far away a light shines
Beyond the hills and pines;
It is lit for me.

BRIDEGROOM
I have thee close, my dear,
No terror can come near;
Only far off the northern light shines clear.

GHOST
Come with me, fair and false,
To our home, come home.
It is my voice that calls:
Once thou wast not afraid
When I woo'd, and said,
'Come, our nest is newly made' –
Now cross the tossing foam.

BRIDE
Hold me one moment longer,
He taunts me with the past,
His clutch is waxing stronger,
Hold me fast, hold me fast.
He draws me from thy heart,
And I cannot withhold:
He bids my spirit depart
With him into the cold:--
Oh bitter vows of old!

新婚与旧鬼

罗赛蒂 著；徐志摩 译

新娘

　　郎呀，郎，抱着我
　　他要把我们拆散；
　　我怕这风狂如虎，
　　与这冷酷的暴烈的海：
　　看呀，那远远的山边，
　　松林里有火光炎炎；
　　那是为我点着的灯台。

新郎

　　你在我的怀里，我爱，
　　谁敢来将你侵犯；
　　那是北极的星芒灿烂。

鬼

　　跟我来，负心的女，
　　回我们家去，回家去
　　这是我的话，我的声
　　我曾经求你的爱，
　　你也曾答我的情，
　　来，我们的安乐窝已经落成
　　快来同登大海的彼岸。

新娘

　　紧紧的楼住我，我的爱
　　他责问我已往的盟约，
　　他抓我的手，扼我的腕，
　　郎呀，休让他将我剽掠。
　　他要剜去你的心头肉，
　　我抵抗他的强暴无法：
　　他指着那阴森的地狱，
　　我心怯他的恫吓：——
　　呀，我摆不脱曾经的盟约！

71

BRIDEGROOM
Lean on me, hide thine eyes:
Only ourselves, earth and skies,
Are present here: be wise.

GHOST
Lean on me, come away,
I will guide and steady:
Come, for I will not stay:
Come, for house and bed are ready.
Ah, sure bed and house,
For better and worse, for life and death:
Goal won with shortened breath:
Come, crown our vows.

BRIDE
One moment, one more word,
While my heart beats still,
While my breath is stirred
By my fainting will.
O friend forsake me not,
Forget not as I forgot:
But keep thy heart for me,
Keep thy faith true and bright;
Through the lone cold winter night
Perhaps I may come to thee.

BRIDEGROOM
Nay peace, my darling, peace:
Let these dreams and terrors cease:
Who spoke of death or change or aught but ease?

新郎
　　偎着我，闭着你的眼：
　　就只你与我，地与天，
　　放心，我爱，再没有祸变。

鬼
　　偎着我，跟着我来，
　　我是你的保护与引导，
　　我不耐烦等着，快来，
　　我们的斩床已经安好。
　　是呀，新的房与新的床，
　　长生不老，我是夫，你是妻，
　　乐园在眼前，只要你的眼闭，
　　来呀，实现盟约的风光。

新娘
　　饶着我，再说一句话，
　　趁我的心血不曾冷，
　　趁我的意志不曾败，
　　趁我的呼吸不曾凉。
　　不要忘记我，我的郎，
　　我便负心，你不要无常，
　　留给我你的心，我的郎君，
　　永保着情真与思缘；
　　在寂寞的冷落的冬夜，
　　我的魂许再来临，我的郎君

新郎
　　定一定心，我爱，安你的神：
　　休教幻梦纠缠你的心灵：
　　那有什么变与死，除了安宁？

GHOST

O fair frail sin,
O poor harvest gathered in!
Thou shalt visit him again
To watch his heart grow cold;
To know the gnawing pain
I knew of old;
To see one much more fair
Fill up the vacant chair,
Fill his heart, his children bear: –
While thou and I together
In the outcast weather
Toss and howl and spin.

鬼

罪孽！脆弱的良心，
这是人们无聊的收成！
你将来重复来临，
只见他的恩情改变，冷淡，
也让你知道那苦痛与怨恨
曾经一度刺戟我的心坎；
只见一个更美而的新人
占据你的房栊，你的床棍，
你的恋爱，与他儿女产生：
那时候你与我，
在晦盲的昏暮
颠播，呼号，纵横。